dal yn barod, Still Ready

Haris Hussnain

BookLeaf Publishing

India | USA | UK

Presentation by *BookLeaf Publishing*

Web: www.bookleafpub.com

E-mail: info@bookleafpub.com

ISBN: 9789360941918

First edition 2024

There are many people who the poems are based on. I dedicate this book to them. Ah but you're making me choose. The poem Not From wonderland is dedicated to my good friend Alice. For those who don't know Alice, she's a friend of mine who is very active in making Wales more accessible for people with disabilities. Big thanks to her for everything she does.

Mae yna lawer o bobl y mae'r cerddi'n seiliedig arnynt. Rwy'n cysegru'r llyfr hwn iddyn nhw. Ah ond rydych chi'n gwneud i mi ddewis. Mae'r gerdd Not From wonderland wedi'i chysegru i fy ffrind da Alice. I'r rhai nad ydynt yn adnabod Alice, mae hi'n ffrind i mi sy'n weithgar iawn yn gwneud Cymru'n fwy hygyrch i bobl ag anableddau. Diolch yn fawr iddi am bopeth mae'n ei wneud.

ACKNOWLEDGEMENT

Well this is an interesting part of a book where I'm meant to thank people. The first thanks goes to the Creative writing society at Cardiff University which is where I was inspired to write and develop my writing skills. The second thanks goes to everyone who read my poems before publication. It's very much appreciated. I would also like to acknowledge Wales's best writers: Jessica Dunrod, Nathan Amin and Bethany Handley who are my heroes and great role models. I read a lot of your work and it really inspired me to finally try creative writing.

Wel dyma ran ddiddorol o lyfr lle dwi i fod i ddiolch i bobl. Mae'r diolch cyntaf yn mynd i'r Gymdeithas Ysgrifennu Creadigol ym Mhrifysgol Caerdydd a dyna lle cefais fy ysbrydoli i ysgrifennu a datblygu fy sgiliau ysgrifennu. Mae'r ail ddiolch yn mynd i bawb a ddarllenodd fy ngherddi cyn eu cyhoeddi. Mae'n cael ei werthfawrogi'n fawr. Hoffwn hefyd gydnabod awduron gorau Cymru: Jessica Dunrod, Nathan Amin a Bethany Handley sef fy arwyr a modelau rôl gwych. Darllenais lawer o'ch gwaith ac fe wnaeth fy ysbrydoli i roi cynnig ar ysgrifennu creadigol o'r diwedd.

PREFACE

The world is an odd place and a lot of things don't make sense and never will make sense. I personally think we should confront some of these worries, doubts and insecurities by finding our voices. Reading is like a room full of silence where one can sit and find comfort.

A big interest of mine is the Welsh language. I grew up in Newport and studied at Cardiff University where I fell in love with the language and went onto learning it. Some of my poems will include Welsh words or be 50% Welsh because I want to connect with my home and the wider community on issues that are affecting us all.

Mae'r byd yn lle od ac nid yw llawer o bethau'n gwneud synnwyr ac ni fyddant byth yn gwneud synnwyr. Yn bersonol, credaf y dylem wynebu rhai o'r pryderon, yr amheuon a'r ansicrwydd hyn trwy ddod o hyd i'n lleisiau. Mae darllen fel ystafell llawn distawrwydd lle gall rhywun eistedd a chael cysur.

Diddordeb mawr i mi yw'r iaith Gymraeg. Cefais fy magu yng Nghasnewydd ac astudiais ym Mhrifysgol Caerdydd lle syrthiais mewn cariad â'r iaith ac es ymlaen i'w dysgu. Bydd rhai o fy ngherddi yn cynnwys geiriau Cymraeg neu fod yn 50% Cymreig oherwydd fy mod eisiau cysylltu gyda fy nghartref a'r gymuned ehangach ar faterion sy'n effeithio ar bob un ohonom.

Alone Wolf and the Willow tree

Normal is not me. I am wild and a freak. I often
wander the woods alone enjoying the peace
and quiet. In the woods, I am free to run
whenever I like.

I can walk across the small foothills to admire
the moon's celestial beauty.

Shining bright
across the woods its white light never intervenes
during the day, like me it is independent.

I must howl at the moon but I chose not to, I am
no shepherd nor a sheep. I am me alone
wolf and free.

I have a purpose and my own beliefs. You can
tell me what to think but I won't listen.

I will never listen. I walk the opposite path in the
woods.

I often see packs in fives and threes walking like
gangsters on a sketchy street.

The other
wolves follow as the alpha leads. This is a
dictatorship but they call it a democracy.
I sometimes join them when they go on a hunt
with their mates.

Their mates take care of them providing food
and meat. But I don't need a mate because I
can get my own food.

I will occasionally meet the pack under the
willow tree.
I will socialise and join in their activities, but
only because I want to.
The pack sometimes squabbles and bickers.

I watch from afar as they behave like animals.
The alpha is now a Shepherd with no sheep,

sitting in the woods like a lemon. What is their
purpose now?

The other pack members are idly sitting in a line
like a squad of soldiers awaiting orders.

With no shepherd, they are lost.
The woods are so quiet, that the pack is trapped
in a stalemate.

I on the other hand am free and proudly gallop
around the woods.

Strange men with hounds enter the woods, are
they searching for me?
I am capable of surviving on my own and I
climb up the tree camouflaged and hidden.

I see the strange men and their hounds walk past
my tree towards the individual pack

members. Their hierarchy fails them and the
men leave with caged wolves.
I could fight with the men and the wolves would
be free, but that is not my destiny.

To many, I am the villain the weirdo the freak,
But, I really am independent, intelligent, free
and not the one caged like a beast on a leash

I am the hero of my story and the writer of my
destiny.

I respected the other wolves and treated them
with kindness, they were mean, cruel vicious
and never self-sufficient.

Their squabbling and fighting is what brought
them to ruin
They didn't respect my individual thoughts,
feelings or wit
But that's ok. When I'm alone a clever idea is
always brewing.

I run across the woods to the willow tree
I climb on top of it watching the midnight scene.

I see the moon shine and I feel a sense of
purpose, Independence and solace. I am my own
hero and I am free.

The Man

Face bruised,

Purple skin from strangulation as a result of a
vile revelation.

Bulging eyes,
skin frayed peeling off as a result of a burn.

Chained up on all fours like a beast one finds on
the Moores.

Mouth gagged, legs bound, and arms tied.
In a dim room with a beast

Who comes out of the night and into the dim
light?

Frightening and stocky build, some call him a
beast, but she calls him a
man.

Purple skin, sharp claws and long hair, she went
from looking like a human to a nightmare.

She roars and screams, moans and sights.
Neighbours think it's an erotic spectacle.

Little do they know none of it was consensual.

y prentis

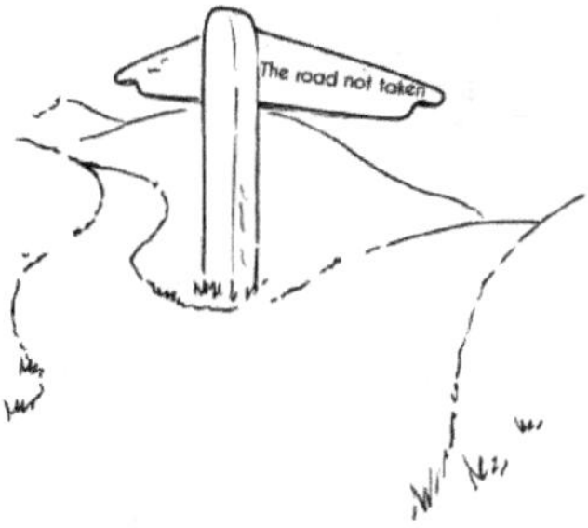

Yr arlunydd
Mae ganddi Nodwyddau yn ei llaw
trywanu trywanu trywanu yn y
croen,

Grym sadistaidd y
ymenydd
Menig ar ddwylo
Manwl a chanolbwyntio
Mae swyddogaethau modur yn achosi straen
iddi.

Lliw rhuddgoch
Disodlwyd gan
du
Lluniadu siapiau a llinellau
Creu darn perffaith o gelf

When the lights go out

Guided by the street lights,
she walks through the night,
not a being in sight.

She can walk peacefully and walk the streets
free.
To do as she pleases.

Suddenly

The lights go out and, guided by the moon,
she makes it out of town.

Strange creatures come out from the bushes,
trying to give her a fright.

They call themselves "men",

but she calls them monsters

They are aggressive and try to force themselves
on her.

She fights back and defends herself .

Her phone camera light gives the rats a fright,
and they go.

scurrying back to their Biffa bins
The green people in flashing cars ignore her
Cries for help.

Statues,
They stare into the darkness,
oblivious to what just happened
They are useless

They call it the "male gaze",
but it's really the plague.
She gets an Uber to take her home

The driver is handsome and gives her a note.
It's his number. She's
Not interested and says,

NO

The handsome face turns into a goblin
that moves its wrinkled green hand up her ankle

She grabs the hand and breaks it.
The Golbin lunges at her,
she punches It falls crying and rolls into a ball.

She cries for Help

A being in green passes by and smiles.
Oblivious to how she's feeling behind those
friendly eyes.

A group of boys help her get home,
wearing red reflective jackets and carrying
torches and phones.

Like kryptonite, the boys keep the monsters
away
they help her through the dark until it's a day
She thanks them and goes to bed.

Dreading the next time she'll have to call them
again
The next day, she sees a being in green dealing
with theft and wonders
Why didn't they help her?

She hears a scream, and another woman is
attacked on the street
moon lighting the scene up.
The being in green,

rather aloof, asks the woman stupid questions
like

Where is the proof?

She looks at him, annoyed and in shock,
as he drives off in his flashy car around the
block.

y dyn eira

Oer, llonydd a marw yw'r dref
Cefais fy magu yn
Stryd dawel, dim ceir
Ddim yn bîp.

Mae gan y dirwedd ddu a llwyd
Trodd i wyn gyda rhyfedd
Creaduriaid eira gyda thrwynau moron yn
goresgyn y stryd.

Mae un yn edrych arnaf gyda'i het Wooly a'i
lygaid botwm.
Yn sydyn iawn maen nhw
a roddir breichiau ffon gan eu
creawdwr

Mae'r dyddiau'n mynd heibio ac mae mwy o'r
creaduriaid rhyfedd hyn yn ymddangos.
Mawr ac aloof, fel gwartheg coll.
Pob cornel stryd dwi'n eu gweld.
Syllu mor farw â'r aer oer.

Maen nhw'n rhyfedd o gymharu â mi.
Edrych yn od a
anffurfiedig.

Rwy'n edrych ar fy nghorff fy hun ac yn
sylweddoli
Yr un ydym ni.
Yr un bodolaeth
Yn oer ac yn unig.

Mae'r haf yn dod a fy ffrind
Diflannu, wedi diflannu'n llwyr.
Ble aethon nhw?
Roedd hi'n Nadolig a doeddwn i ddim
Yn unig.

Ond, nawr ydw i
Yn unig.

ein un ni o hyd

I lawer o bobl
mae chwiliad
Am dŷ!
Nid fy nhŷ i yw Caerdydd ond dyma'r lle rwy'n
ei alw
Diogel!

Caerdydd yw sut y gwnaethom ni
Dinas cariad heb unrhyw ffiniau
Lle gall gwerin o bob math gerdded
Dal dwylo'n ddiogel.

Rhyw ddydd yn y dre
Dw i'n mynd i wylio'r bandiau
Mae'n ddinas o synau
Lle nad yw cariad yn gwybod unrhyw derfynau

Nid yw Caerdydd yn imiwn i'r hyn rwy'n ei alw
Helgwn.
Maen nhw'n ceisio ein dal mewn cadwyni
Ac ailosod y cyflymder.
Ynghyd â'n calonnau a'n synau
Rydym yn cynhyrchu'r alaw berffaith i
Gwahardd nhw allan.

Dyma Gaerdydd
ein cartref
Ein coron.

Meeting Santa

It is Christmas Eve and I cannot sleep.
I hear a noise, a voice
I hear a creep
Ho, ho, ho
I hear at night.
Is it my son crying?
Is it my wife laughing?

Ho, ho, ho I hear again
I walk down the wooden stairs
Creek, creek.
I hear the noise again.

Standing infront of me is
A strange creature.
Big, big, big creature.
Human in face with horns
Carrying a mace.

Grrr he says to me his voice
Full of malice with his mouth like an
Angry dog about to attack.
Next to him is a small creature
Hideous in appearance.
Pointy ears, crooked teeth.

I look at it and it looks at me
I tell them to leave, tell them to go
The demonic creatures go
No, ho, ho, ho.

The clock strikes 12
The creature scurries up the chimney
My son hurries downstairs.
Milk and cookies in hand waiting for Santa.

He waited and waited but nobody
Came.
Who was that earlier?
That creature full of anger?
Was he the famous Santa

Spiritual leader

A Being with a beard
Walks like a beast
Talks like a moron.

Shouts real eerie
Scares the living
Daylight out of me.

What they say
Is used against me

Community leaders
I scoff at that though
People look up to them all foolish and naive

with no true meaning, soul its like the monster
has drained then of their
soul

nobody cares
Doomed, doomed
Bearded being

Invincible, unstoppable
Planning his next

Invasion

With his sleeper
Agents.

Beware
Stay safe

Keep your distance
If you ever see this creature

Then run.

Dragonism

The primaeval age saw the rise and fall of the
dragon empire.
Scarlet dragons stood for justice and leadership.
They sought to unite the other fighting mortals
of the primaeval era
 with their pacifistic beliefs, peace, and harmony.

Other creatures marvelled at the sight of their
scarlet scales and the sound of the melodic
language they spoke. Dragons lived in a golden
city that was so bright it could be seen from
space. Its sight would attract angels who would
come to sing with the dragons upon their golden
spires that overlooked the rest of the earth.
Asserting tyranny

The 25th-century person knows little about the
golden city, nor do they understand what
tragedies happened there. During one winter, the
dragons invited the mortal races to join them in a
melee tournament. A ritualistic form of
entertainment that was popular with primaeval
beings. They asked the wealthiest humans to
watch the tournament or, should I say,
bloodshed.

Many people were enslaved and instructed to build the tournament grounds for the melee next to the golden city. Throughout the city, one can hear the dragons singing their peaceful, angelic song. If you were to venture to the slave camps, you could hear the screams of builders as they starved to death, the sound of structures flattening workers and the sound of the axe executing those who spoke out. Dragons would hunt the vibrant mermaids and colourful unicorns that came to watch the tournament. They were massacred

The dragon's voices dominated the lands, cancelling out the screams of victims. The golden city is so bright that it prevents mortals from seeing the crimson blood-filled ocean of skeletal remains. Rarely do mortals find the red oceans. When they do
They are silenced.

On occasion, restless spirits torment the dragons driving them to insanity
eventialiy this devolved their people and made their city into ruins that the mortal people plundered. Blood money!
A nation built by slaves.

The dragon's legacy lives on through the
selfishness and greed of mortal beings. The
dragons and their vanity, double standards, greed
and demand for entertainment.
Scales of crimson red singing their dirge-like
song What's the difference between them and the
mortal Edward Colston now?

The Gardner and his daughter

We Grow old like a plant withering.
The plant starts as a seed
Small and delicate, the size of a grain of rice.

Small and innocent like a child.
The garnder tends to this seed like a parent tends
to child.
Nurturing and loving the beautiful
Thing.

The plant faces a dangerous quest.
It must survive the harsh, barren land
Predatory Insects come go Plant.
They try to hurt her.
No! Says the Gardner
With his shovel he squashes them
They go pop like a head in a guillotine.

In the colder months Plant has her home
flooded.
The kind Gardner let's her inside.
She blooms, she blossoms.
His plant is growing up so fast.

On a stormy evening the farmer dies.

Sirens get louder.
Neeenaw neenaw.
Plant is sad, her vibrant colours fade
She starts to slouch.
She dies, dead.

A vibrant light appears
Wooooosh.
A mysterious force takes Plant up to the sky.
She wakes up next to the gardener.
Loving and nurturing her.

I think this is a matter of life
or theft

Everything was once green, trees, plants and
leaves.
Everyone could breath

Sometimes warm, and Sometimes
the occasional storm
back then, heat, rain and thunder
every day was never the
Norm.

The days have gone when one could
walk outside down a street
full of green and breath the fresh air.
Now everyone is like a zombie.
The atmosphere is
Blue.

The air is like poison filled with
toxins released by the goblin Princes.
They play monopoly with planet Earth.
Everything they touch turns blue.

They offer a sacrifice to their goblin king.
Burning the earth's treasures. They receive gold.

They drain the planet turning Earth.
Blue.

They have destroyed the lives of many.
The goblins enslave not everyone.
Some manage to break free and
heal the world that has been hurt.
Despite every obstacle, the goblins
won't back down, scratching their rubbery green chins
and bathing in
gold.

The once vibrant green world of Earth had
ife and happiness.
The current world of the earth has sadness
resembling a post-apocalyptic
scene.

The world is turning Blue with all we know
becoming sea.
Join a team, hunt the greedy creatures and
turn our planet
green.

Not from Wonderland

Blonde hair, bright smile
She walks with her shoulders back with a
humble smile.
Her heart stretches a thousand miles.
She runs with the swans and forms a bond.

Warrior,
Fighting strange creatures in blue suits.
These strange creatures are ugly.
They are green, miserable and everywhere.
They take over Cardiff with a firm hand.
Killing, destroying everything devastating,
eradicating.
Our Blonde hero kills them.
Her words destroying them, her words
disintegrate them.
She raises an army of red people.
Brave and reckless, ready to fight.
They travel to the centre.
Riding a giant dog who flattens the ugly alien
scum.
Our hero approaches them ready to speak.

Blabba blabba.

A strange language comes from their mouth-like
appendage.
She extends her arm out for a handshake
For peace.
They say, NO!
They say war
She say GO!

With a click of her fingers
A rabbit hole appears.
It sucks the aliens in.
Sluuuuuuuuwwwwwpppppp
Until a load flash and bang.
The hole closes.

Many thank our hero.
Including a stripy cat.
She sees our hero's hat and extends her hand.
Dear hero are you from wonderland.
No she replies.
My home is Earth.

The cat looks sad, she says
I'm all alone.
Our hero invites her for tea and a scone.
They go home and talk about life.
Counting all the cathays mice.

Freaks

Creature,

Dark hair, dark eyes
Presenter and leader.
5ft tall

This is the politician.
She wakes up from her master bedroom.
The maid comes running in fast.
With enough food to feed an army.
The politician appears so sweet.
Handbag in hand, handing stickers to children.
Visits the hospital, visits the street
But behind closed doors what does she do

Under the sheets.
At the end of a long day she arrives hone.
Where she is looking for a partner on the phone.
A man appears in suit and tie.
Oops, he forgets to do up his fly.
She catches notice and pretends not to die.
Only a fool couldn't notice the red tinge in her
eyes.
They go upstairs to her room.
Calling the maid.

The maid enters all confused as they tie her up
to a broom.
She watches in horror as the two
Strip to their undies.
Sexy and model-like is the politician and her
partner dominating the maid with their looks.

The maid is confused.
The politician sighs before giving the maid a
nasty bite.
The maid screams for her life.
Seeing the red in the politician's eyes.
They kill the maid and eat her whole.
Before removing their human skin suit.
In truth, the politician and her partner are green,
scally like a crocodile with teeth like a vampire.
Eyes red like blood.
The creatures give a menacing laugh.
The next day the cycle starts again.
Another hardworking, innocent person is hired
ad the maid.
Used and abused.

Boring squiggly

The Earth,
Planet of colours,
Vibrant beautiful colours.
In school children would marvel at
The colours and their beauty.
Keeping the Earth colourful
Was their duty.

That duty has since become a
Right
That was lost to the knights and their
Giant Eraser.

The colour Green,
nonexistent in my small town.
Replaced by grey, stone and brick.
The plants scream as they are slaughtered by
strange creatures with multiple teeth that roll
across the feild.

The colour Red,
Ever so present.
The rivers and oceans are a deep crimson
The skeletal sharks and dolphins populate the
ocean.

Disease and decay
Are the norm of today.

The colour Yellow,
Toxic and poisonous
A common colour where I live.
Illness and danger.
No longer the happy, sunny warm
Colour it once was.

The colour Blue,
Morbid and bleak,
Seeing blue is like seeing a seagul.
Scaverging with nothing in its beek.
Once a colour of oceans and sea.
No the colour of bed ridden Disease.
Despair.

The colour pink,
Psychotic and insane,
Once a symbol of feminimity.
Punk rock and rebellious people.
Now the symbol of insanity.

Black,
No even a colour just a shade,
But in recent years its a colour
It has earned its name.
Everyday darkness,

Everyday silence,
There is nothing.
Nothing left of the colourful vibrant Earth.

Only
Darkness

Resurgence of the Soul: A New Year's Ode

In the silence of the midnight chime,
A new year unfolds, marking the time.
Yet shadows linger, heavy and deep,
Where whispers of sadness, their secrets keep.

Beneath the fireworks' dazzling spree,
A soul in sorrow, chained, not free.
The weight of the past, a burden to bear,
In the cold embrace of the midnight air.

The calendar turns, pages crisp and clean,
Yet in the heart's chambers, a somber scene.
Depression's tendrils, a relentless hold,
A tale untold, in the shadows, bold.

Each step forward, a weary march,
Through the graveyard of dreams, in the dark.
But in the quietude, a flicker appears,
A glimmer of hope, dispelling the fears.

The clock's ticking echoes in the mind,
A reminder of moments left behind.
Yet amid the sadness, a phoenix may rise,
From the ashes of despair, a soul's reprise.

Death's shadow hovers, a specter near,
Yet life persists, casting away the fear.
In the tapestry of time, threads intertwine,
A delicate dance, both yours and mine.

The moonlight weaves tales of joy and woe,
A symphony of emotions in the ebb and flow.
Through tears that fall like winter's rain,
A promise of healing, a latent gain.

As the stars cascade in the vast expanse,
A celestial dance, a cosmic chance.
In the abyss of despair, a spark of light,
Guiding us through the endless night.

Though the path may seem desolate and steep,
A new year whispers, encouraging us to leap.
For in the union of sorrow and hope,
Lies the strength to cope, to truly elope.

So let the verses of this poem unfold,
A tapestry of emotions, both young and old.
For in the crucible of pain and mirth,
We find the essence of our rebirth.

Eclipsed Blooms

In the garden of shadows where moonlight
wanes,
Blossoms of blood, entwined with sinister
strains.
A tale unfolds, a macabre ballet,
Where love and death waltz in the pale spring's
sway.

Beneath the boughs where the nightbirds sing,
Echoes of footsteps, a clandestine fling.
Lover's whispers, an eerie refrain,
As the air fills with the scent of impending pain.

Crimson petals unfurl in the midnight air,
The symphony of anguish, a ghastly affair.
Murderous tendrils, like vines they entwine,
As the moon bears witness to the sinister design.

Gory echoes paint the moonlit scene,
A tableau of horror, where nightmares convene.
Love, a phantom that dances on the graves,
In the crypt of desire, where the lost heart
craves.

Gothic spires rise in the haunted mist,

A silhouette of doom where the lovers kissed.
Bats in flight, with wings of ebony,
Dark serenades sung in the tragic lea.

The springtime blooms in hues of despair,
As love metamorphoses into a nightmarish glare.
Gothic cathedrals, adorned in gloom,
Witness the union of love and doom.

A tapestry woven with threads of dread,
Where passion bleeds and the roses are red.
In the garden of shadows, where the crows caw,
Love and gore entwine in a macabre ballet's
draw.

Beware the vernal embrace, a sinister hug,
Where the petals weep and the tombstones
shrug.
Spring's rebirth, a melancholy spree,
As love and darkness merge in unholy glee

Goat

In January's grasp, where frost doth cling,
A tale unfolds of an ancient being.
A creature cloaked in myth and fur,
The goat, a symbol, both kind and infer.

In shadows cast by winter's pale moon,
The caprine spirit begins its tune.
With cloven hooves upon frozen ground,
It treads the path where legends abound.

A creature, oft feared, by superstition's plight,
A symbol in myths, both darkness and light.
Pan, the horned one, in wild pursuit,
Dances 'neath winter's starlit flute.

The goat, a creature with eyes of gold,
In January's frosty hold.
A symbol of nature, untamed and free,
Yet draped in whispers of dark decree.

For in ancient tales, the goat was tied,
To rituals where shadows hide.
A scapegoat, bearing sins untold,
In the grasp of evil, a story unfolds.

Yet, in fairness, the goat bears grace,
A creature of earth, a sacred space.
A guardian of myths, a symbol profound,
In January's frosty playground.

Horns that curl like winter vines,
A creature ancient, where myth entwines.
Evil's guise, a mere facade,
As the goat ambles, in nature's ode.

So, in January's cold embrace,
Reflect upon the goat's mystic grace.
A symbol not wholly of evil's kin,
But a creature ancient, untamed within

The willow

Beneath the soft caress of spring's embrace,
Willow trees dance with delicate grace.
Their branches, like weeping tendrils, sway,
In the vernal breeze, a verdant ballet.

Silken leaves in hues of tender green,
Unfurling like secrets once unseen.
A canopy of whispers, soft and low,
As the willow weaves tales of long ago.

Graceful limbs, a cascade of sorrow,
Yet within, a resilience to borrow.
As winter's grasp begins to wane,
The willow's spirit rises, free from chains.

A riverbank's companion, silent and wise,
Reflecting in waters, beneath azure skies.
Gently dipping branches in the stream,
The willow, a muse in a tranquil dream.

In the tapestry of spring, a story unfolds,
Where the willow's tale, like nature, molds.
With each bud that bursts in vibrant glee,
The willow hums a song of jubilee.

Through April showers and May's sweet bloom,
The willow casts away winter's gloom.
Its leaves like cascading tears of joy,
Nature's masterpiece, without alloy.

Whispers of the breeze, a lullaby,
As willow branches brush the sky.
A testament to endurance, evergreen,
In the rebirth of spring, a timeless scene.

So, beneath the canvas of cerulean hue,
The willow dances, its spirit anew.
In spring's tender grasp, a verdant spree,
A symphony of life, the willow tree.

Mari

In Wales, where winter winds entwine,
A specter roams, Mari Lwyd, divine.
A mare of bones, a skull aglow,
In ancient rituals, its tales do flow.

With ribbons fluttering in the breeze,
Mari Lwyd dances through villages with ease.
A phantom steed of yesteryear,
Whispering secrets, the living to endear.

Beneath the moon's soft argent gleam,
The Mari's presence, a spectral dream.
Adorned with ribbons, colors bright,
Against the canvas of a starlit night.

In doorways, it stands, a spectral guest,
A challenge issued in rhyming zest.
A merry exchange, living and the dead,
In Mari's dance, tradition is bred.

The skull, a lantern in the winter's gloom,
Illuminating tales in the chilly room.
A bridge between realms, unseen and known,
Mari Lwyd's magic in tradition sown.

Through ale-filled mirth, the night unfolds,
As Mari Lwyd's tales are retold.
A fusion of laughter, spirit, and cheer,
Welsh hearts warmed in winter's sphere.

In this spectral ballet, ancient and bright,
Mari Lwyd dances through the night.
A guardian of tradition, bones and grace,
Guiding Wales through winter's embrace

Ugly men

In shadows cast by life's cruel jest,
A tale unfolds of men distressed.
Faces etched with lines of sorrow,
In the silent realms where sadness burrows.

Ugly, not in form, but in despair,
Their hearts heavy with burdens to bear.
Eyes that mirror a world unkind,
Reflecting the wounds left behind.

In the tapestry of life, a somber hue,
These men carry stories, not seen by view.
Fragments of pain, etched on their skin,
In the quiet struggle where they've been.

Their laughter muted, a melancholic sound,
In the echoes of sorrows, they are bound.
Yet within the shadows, beauty may hide,
A resilience found in the tears they've cried.

Ugliness, a label unjustly worn,
In a world where judgments are harshly borne.
For in the depth of their melancholy gaze,
Lie untold chapters, life's intricate maze.

In their solitude, they find their art,
A canvas painted with the hues of heart.
Ugly, not in essence, but in the world's cruel
gaze,
Yet within, resilience and strength amaze.

So let us not judge by external decree,
The sad, so-called "ugly" men we see.
For within each soul, a story unfolds,
Of battles fought, and strength that molds.

Rex

In the shadows of a twisted throne,
An evil king claims a kingdom his own.
Crowned in darkness, his scepter cruel,
A tyrant's rule, a heart turned to fuel.

His eyes, like ember, blaze with scorn,
A ruler born where shadows are born.
Ambition twisted, a malevolent scheme,
In the corridors of power, a venomous dream.

Upon his brow, a sinister crown,
Woven with deceit, tyranny renown.
A kingdom enslaved in chains of dread,
Under the rule of the king with a heart like lead.

His laughter echoes in the dungeons deep,
Where secrets whispered, the oppressed still
weep.
A realm in darkness, under his command,
An evil king with an iron hand.

He builds his empire on deceit's foundation,
A despot's reign, a cruel narration.
Injustice blooms like poisonous flowers,
Fed by the king's unholy powers.

In the court, where lies are spun,
The evil king's decree, a tale begun.
A puppet master in a wicked dance,
Weaving destruction, malevolence enhance.

Yet, in the whispers of rebellion's breath,
A flicker of hope against the king's dark depth.
For empires built on shadows and fear,
Are destined to crumble when justice draws
near.

In the annals of time, his legacy etched,
The evil king, whose power stretched.
A cautionary tale of the darkened throne,
Where cruelty reaps what it has sown.

www.ingramcontent.com/pod-product-compliance
Lightning Source LLC
LaVergne TN
LVHW021255200726
843509LV00012B/1676